Journeying with Jesus
A Lenten Study for Adults

Reginald Mallett

Abingdon Press
Nashville

JOURNEYING WITH JESUS
A LENTEN STUDY FOR ADULTS

Copyright © 1996 by Abingdon Press

All rights reserved.
No part of this work may be reproduced or transmitted in any form or by any means, electronic or mechanical, including photocopying and recording, or by any information storage or retrieval system, except as may be expressly permitted by the 1976 Copyright Act or in writing from the publisher. Requests for permission should be addressed to Abingdon Press, P.O. Box 801, 201 Eighth Avenue South, Nashville, TN 37202-0801.

This book is printed on recycled, acid-free paper.

Library of Congress Cataloging-in-Publication Data

Mallett, Reginald.
    Journeying with Jesus : a Lenten study for adults / Reginald Mallett.
       p. cm.
    ISBN 0-687-03538-4 (pbk. : alk. paper)
    1. Lent—Prayer-books and devotions—English. 2. Jesus Christ—Prayer-books and devotions—English. I. Title.
BV85.M245   1996
242'.34—dc20   95-31230
                                                                        CIP

Except for brief paraphrases or unless otherwise noted, scripture quotations are from the New Revised Standard Version Bible, Copyright 1989 by the Division of Christian Education of the National Council of the Churches of Christ in the USA. Used by permission.

That noted J. B. Phillips is from *The New Testament in Modern English,* rev. ed. (New York: Macmillan, 1972). Copyright © J. B. Phillips, 1958, 1959, 1960, 1972.

That noted KJV is from the Authorized or King James Version of the Bible.

The excerpt from John Masefield's "Everlasting Mercy" (p. 46) is printed by permission of the Society of Authors as the literary representative of the Estate of John Masefield.

96 97 98 99 00 01 02 03 04 05 — 10 9 8 7 6 5 4 3 2 1

MANUFACTURED IN THE UNITED STATES OF AMERICA

Contents

Introduction
Lent: A Time for Journeying with Jesus 5

The First Week in Lent
The Wilderness Questions (Preparing) 6

The Second Week in Lent
Second-Rate Instruments but First-Rate Music (Becoming Disciples) . . .13

The Third Week in Lent
Doing the Best Things at the Worst Times (Accepting the Challenge) . . .19

The Fourth Week in Lent
Reflections of Jesus (Being Healed) 26

The Fifth Week in Lent
The Mountain and the Valley (Gathering Strength) 32

The Sixth Week in Lent
The Cry of Human Need (Meditating on His Suffering) 37

The Seventh Week in Lent
Fear and Joy (Easter People) 43

To Mark, Elizabeth,
and their families,
with love

Introduction
Lent: A Time for Journeying with Jesus

For Christians, Lent provides an opportunity for reflection. It is a time when we are encouraged to trace the footsteps of Jesus. In one sense it is a solemn time. The curtain rises on Ash Wednesday, a day that is marked with penitence. It is a time when we share Paul's ambition: "I want to know Christ and the power of his resurrection and the fellowship of sharing in his sufferings, by becoming like him in his death" (Phil. 3:10). Our Lenten journey takes us to Gethsemane, to betrayal, rejection, and crucifixion.

And yet Lent is also a time for gladness and inspiration. The concluding chapter is an open tomb and a shout of acclamation. Through the darkness we come to the glorious light of Easter day and the wonder of resurrection. Journey's end is a glorified Savior proclaiming, "All authority in heaven and on earth has been given to me. Therefore go and make disciples of all nations" (Matt. 28:18-19).

Come, let us sit at the feet of the Master, see the world and its need through those eyes of compassion, discover afresh that all-inclusive invitation to follow, stand in awe under the shadow of the cross, and exult in the glory and wonder of resurrection. Jesus invites us not only to a journey of devotion but also to an exciting adventure in thought. Traveling with Jesus is not for the faint-hearted. It is to leave the comfortable coastal harbor that the trembling vessels of our lives love to hug, and to put out boldly into the depths of the sea of thought and truth and be carried out of our depths. Our only security is Christ, and our only hope is God's free grace. But by having the inner courage and determination to make this journey, we make new discoveries about our Savior and ourselves, and the wonder of death and resurrection is made all the more complete.

The First Week in Lent
The Wilderness Questions (Preparing)

> *In those days Jesus came from Nazareth of Galilee and was baptized by John in the Jordan. . . . And the Spirit immediately drove him out into the wilderness. He was in the wilderness forty days, tempted by Satan; and he was with the wild beasts; and the angels waited on him. (Mark 1:9, 12-13)*

"I suggest we wait. I don't think he is ready for it just now," the senior physician said.

I was in my last week as a junior doctor in that hospital. We were discussing one of the patients, a young man aged twenty-seven who had been admitted several weeks earlier. He had no immediate family and very few visitors. He and I often chatted when things were quiet, and we found that in our Christian faith we had a great deal in common. On that day the last tests had been completed and the diagnosis finally made. He had a slowly progressive condition which, sadly, was terminal.

It is always difficult to decide when is the best time to break this kind of news to a patient. No two individuals are alike, and such a decision requires sensitive clinical judgment. If anyone could get it right, it would be the senior physician whom I was assisting. He was a man of great compassion, deep faith, and rare sensitivity. I valued his vast experience and wisdom, and on this occasion I took his advice. I deferred the breaking of the bad news.

According to plans already made, shortly after that conversation with my "chief," I moved to medical work in another area. A year later, out of the blue, a letter arrived from this patient. In it he told me on a follow-up visit to the out-patients department he had been left alone to wait for the specialist. On a table in front of him was his file. He had been unable to resist the temptation to look. Flicking through the pages he came across my case summary with its grim conclusion. It was this which had prompted his letter.

Frankly I expected a chiding. I could not have been more wrong. The letter overflowed with gratitude. He thanked me for not telling him what his condition was at the time. My chief had been right. "I wasn't ready for it," he explained. "I have needed this past year to go on a pilgrimage of inward exploration and face the Wilderness Questions." By the time he had peeped into the folder, he had made that spiritual journey and was ready.

"*The Wilderness Questions.*" The phrase still echoes in my mind.

I wonder why Jesus shared this intensely personal story about his Wilderness Questions with the disciples? The information could have come from no one else. Jesus was alone when he wrestled with his inner questioning. That titanic struggle was seen by none but God. Were the disciples admitted into this privileged personal experience because the principles at stake were so fundamental? Was it necessary for them to understand what happened out there in the solitude in order to make sense of their journey with Jesus?

Temptations are very personal. They are peculiarly suited to our dreams, ambitions, and aspirations. The greater a person's potential and gifts, the more powerful are the temptations that they arouse. The temptation of the orator with the ability to stir minds and hearts with glowing words differs from that of the scientist with an inventive mind or the musician with talented fingers. What is seen as life's supreme goal determines what an individual's temptation is.

For Jesus, the supreme end was to bring in the kingdom of God. In the wilderness he struggled with three fundamental questions. Since those who seek to be disciples are called to pursue that same end, they must necessarily face those same concerns. The Wilderness Questions are a necessary starting point as we journey through Lent to Calvary and Easter.

Wilderness Question #1: Can we live by bread alone?

"If you are the Son of God, command these stones to become loaves of bread." But he [Jesus] answered, "It is written, 'One does not live by bread alone, / but by every word that comes from the mouth of God.' " (Matt. 4:3-4)

Have you noticed how, when you are on a diet, your mind, like the compass needle seeking the magnetic north, always seems to come back to food? You are walking through town feeling hungry, and suddenly you are overpowered by the irresistibly delicious aroma of fresh bread coming from a nearby bakery. You are sitting on a park bench when someone walks by eating a snack, and wafting on the breeze come the unmistakable savory delights of hamburger or fried chicken. To escape from these allures you retreat to your home and watch television. And there the scene is a restaurant where the principal characters are devouring a most enticing meal. It is as though there is a universal conspiracy dedicated to breaking your resolve.

It was likely that, after a time of fasting, Jesus looked at the smooth, flat stones in the wilderness and immediately thought about the loaves that Mary used to bake in Nazareth. And then almost immediately there would have come a larger vision. He would have seen that he was not alone in his hunger. Before him would have stretched the vision of a world crying out for bread. Why not use his powers to feed himself and the rest of humanity?

In his hunger Jesus became one with the starving of the world; one with the hungry in the Roman Empire; one with the children pleading for food in Bangladesh, Ethiopia, Bosnia; one with the emaciated beggars dying on the streets of Calcutta. With such an exquisitely sensitive nature, Jesus surely saw such hunger not only as an offense against humanity but also as an offense against God. The knowledge that, in God's world of plenty, some were dying from lack of bread while others had so much that they threw it away would be to him nothing less than blasphemy.

We talk about "saving souls." Jesus is much more radical. He refuses to separate souls from bodies. He comes to save not just a part of humanity but the whole. He comes to save men and women in the totality of their being. The Christian life is not just one of prayer and personal devotion to God. It also involves feeding the hungry and caring for the sick, for "just as you did it to one of the least of these . . . you did it to me" (Matt. 25:40).

Who is that foolish man risking pneumonia, trudging ankle-deep through the snow slush of a London January begging on behalf of the poor? Why, it is ardent evangelist John Wesley at the age of eighty-four! (see Wesley's *Journal,* vol. 7, p. 42; Epworth Press, 1938). No one in England had a greater passion for souls than he. And no one had a more all-consuming desire to feed the hungry and clothe the naked. There was no artificial separation of humankind into souls and bodies for him.

Yet here there are perilous waters that we must navigate with care. Political creeds and ideologies have been based on the false supposition that since we are not able to live without bread, then bread is what we must have—and nothing more. But are we just another species of animal? Are we just bodies that need food and warmth, that flourish, reproduce, and then wither away like grass? In his ringing answer to this first Wilderness Question, the word of Jesus is as clear as a bell. Humankind is infinitely more. It may be possible to *exist* by bread alone, but that is not the same as living. More than bread is necessary if we are to be fully and gloriously alive. If we are to live abundantly, if we are to rise to the God-intended heights of our humanity, then we need the dimension and the food of heaven. We need every word that proceeds from the mouth of God.

This first Wilderness Question addresses the nature of being. Our lives can be truly understood, evaluated, fulfilled, and satisfied—they can rise to their full stature—only when they become part of God's eternal plan. And this happens when they are sustained not merely by the bread of earth, important though that be, but also by the bread of heaven. By every word that comes from the mouth of God.

Wilderness Question #2: Are we to believe without proof?

"If you are the Son of God, throw yourself down; for it is written, 'He will command his angels concerning you.' " . . . Jesus said to him, "Again it is written, 'Do not put the Lord your God to the test.' " (Matt. 4:6-7)

In my first year in seminary, one of our required courses was psychology. One day in class we discussed hypnosis, and we discovered that our professor occasionally practiced it. Some classmates were skeptical about the genuineness of the hypnotic state. In response to our request, the professor agreed to give a demonstration that afternoon.

Word of what was about to happen soon spread around the seminary. When the hour arrived, the room was crowded. A volunteer was called for, and one of the outspoken skeptics stepped forward, confident that he would prove it all to be nonsense. The teacher used no lights or swaying pendants. His finger moved forward and backward rhythmically for less than thirty seconds, and our classmate was gone! Completely hypnotized.

Then the professor offered us several proofs of the depth of the trance. He asked our colleague to lie across three chairs; one at his head, one at his feet, and the other supporting the rest of his body. Using the power of suggestion, he persuaded the subject that his body was becoming as rigid as a block of stone; and sure enough that's what happened. The professor then had the middle chair taken away so that the student was suspended only by his neck and his feet. Two other students were then invited to sit on the hypnotized subject's chest, and they did! His body remained rigid all the time.

After a number of similar demonstrations, our classmate was brought round. He could not recall anything of what had happened, but the rest of us would never forget it. Any lingering doubt we had about hypnosis was gone.

There is something very reassuring about that kind of proof; actually to see and touch. Most of us at one time or another long for such certainty; it is part of our human condition. How encouraging to know that in assuming the mantle of humanity, even the Savior was not immune from this kind of longing. If he were to fling himself from the pinnacle of the temple, such a spectacular rescue not only would dazzle others to faith but would also prove *to himself* who he was. This was a most subtle temptation. "If you are the Son of God, then prove it both to yourself and the world, once and for all. Throw yourself from a pinnacle of the temple. When God intervenes and rescues you, all doubt in your or anyone else's mind will be gone."

The tension between faith and doubt is the product of our humanity. We long for certitude, for some sort of spiritual sensation that will serve as a kind of proof. It is not that we want to be dazzled by stunts. There are deeper places in our hearts than that. There are dark days when we are disappointed, hurt, battered, frightened, or even overwhelmed by a sense of dread and depression. We long to be convinced that out there in that darkness is a gracious, kind, and providential hand. Then we can face the future with cool and steady eyes. Is this such an unreasonable desire?

The fundamental weakness of this kind of faith that rests in "evidence" and "proof" is that although it may excite our wonder, it doesn't change our hearts or make us better. All through his ministry Jesus was surrounded by those who wanted him to give them a sign. But the mission of Jesus was not to dazzle men and women with wonders. It was to show them the loving heart of a God to whom they could be reconciled. And this new relationship that he made possible required trust, based not upon a stunt but on the nature of God.

To journey with Jesus is to explore a faith that is buttressed not by artificial aids but by love and a childlike trust.

Wilderness Question #3: Can we serve God and ourselves?

The devil took him to a very high mountain and showed him all the kingdoms of the world and their splendor; and he said to him, "All these I will give you, if you will fall down and worship me." Jesus said to him, "Away with you, Satan! for it is written, 'Worship the Lord your God, and serve only him.' " (Matt. 4:8-10)

The answer of Jesus to this third Wilderness Question, underlined by his uncompromising life, is that heaven's objectives can be achieved only by heaven's methods. We have to choose between serving God and serving ourselves.

Colin G. Evans in his book *A Month of Sundays* (London: Independent

Press, 1964, p. 119), quotes a preacher who linked together two biblical texts, both of which record human achievements:

> Now Absalom in his lifetime had taken and set up for himself a pillar that is in the King's Valley . . . ; he called the pillar by his own name. It is called Absalom's Monument to this day. (2 Sam. 18:18)
> So he [Jesus] came to a Samaritan city called Sychar, near the plot of ground that Jacob had given to his son Joseph. Jacob's well was there.
> (John 4:5-6)

A pillar and a well. A memorial in stone and a memorial in water. Absalom's pillar was for selfish ends, to perpetuate his own glory. Ironically, it has long since disappeared in the sands of time. Jacob's well was intended for others besides the patriarch himself and his immediate family. It was to serve the wider community. Generations would be blessed by it, and, in the fullness of time, the Savior of the world would ask for a drink of its water. Heaven's method is that of self-giving and service. That method alone will accomplish heaven's objective, which is the transformation of human life and the ushering in of a kingdom of love and community.

We sometimes say that someone "rises to the occasion," but we are wrong. The occasion merely provides an opportunity for character to be revealed. There are times when, like our Master, we find ourselves on that high mountain. Before us are some of the world's prizes, and they look glittering and desirable. It is easy to be beguiled by the inviting sights arrayed before us. Many of us are deceived and reach out for power, possessions, and influence. We erect our pillars. We accept the world's methods and, perhaps, prove successful in gaining some of those dazzling rewards. In building our pillars we may receive all kinds of applause, for ours is a sycophantic age that worships success.

But, thank God, there are some who choose to travel with Jesus and use heaven's methods to achieve heaven's objectives. It is a narrow and hard way. Instead of self-seeking and erecting a pillar to their own glory, they choose a life of service; digging a well for the benefit of others. Often they receive little congratulation, but behind them they leave a generation refreshed because they traveled that way. And best of all, they hear the Master's voice: "Well done good and faithful servant."

This Lent, Jesus calls us to journey with him. And that means facing the Wilderness Questions.

Study Questions

1. Read Psalm 51. This well-known expression of penitence is often used in services of worship and is particularly appropriate at the beginning of Lent when it is most helpful in self-examination. Find time to reflect on each verse in the psalm and let it become your prayer. If God is to create a clean heart in you (v. 10), what are the things that will have to be removed from your life?

2. What are the most difficult temptations you have to face as you journey with Jesus? Each of us will have a different list. What strategies have *you* devised for coping with them?

3. Jesus reminds us that we cannot live spiritually by bread alone. At the same time, however, he does not ignore the fact that we cannot live physically without bread (Matt. 25:31-40). How can we as God's people make sure that we care for the physical needs of our neighbors and yet at the same time hold in balance our supreme need for spiritual food? What specific things can you do?

4. Read John 6:22-40. What do you find most helpful in providing you with "the bread of life" (v. 35)? Is it worship, the sacrament of Holy Communion, a Sunday school class, a time of private devotion, or some other means? Have you ever shared this with anyone else? If not, why not? Someone may be hungering and need your help.

5. Have you ever been tempted to ask God for some tangible proof, some outward demonstration that would reinforce your faith? (Read Matt. 4:5-7 again.) What has helped you most in overcoming this temptation? How would you respond to someone who said, "I will believe in God if my loved one is restored to physical health once more"?

Focus for the Week: Self-examination

Your Lenten journey with Jesus is meaningful only if you are absolutely honest with yourself and with God. Consider what may have hindered your discipleship and made your witness for Christ less effective. Resolve that during this Lenten journey you will explore your awareness of God's work in your life and, by meditating on Christ, will allow yourself to be drawn into the heart of God.

The Second Week in Lent
Second-Rate Instruments but First-Rate Music (Becoming Disciples)

Blessed are you, Simon son of Jonah! . . . And I tell you, you are Peter, and on this rock I will build my church, and the gates of Hades will not prevail against it.
(Matt. 16:17-18)

What does it take to become a disciple? As a teenager I heard a visiting preacher tell a story about a distinguished violinist. Apparently, in one particular city envious critics of the performer circulated derogatory rumors. "It is not his skill that produces the beautiful music," they murmured. "Anyone could do what he does with such a violin as his. It is not he who deserves the credit but Antonio Stradivari." These unkind whispers reached the ear of the violinist.

His next appearance in that city was at a symphony concert where he was to play the lead in a performance of Mendelssohn's violin concerto. He played as one inspired, and the listeners were enraptured. After the triumphant finale, the audience erupted into prolonged applause. The violinist acknowledged their tribute. When the cheering died away, he made a brief statement. "Some have said that my music is due to Stradivari's instrument. It is true that it does indeed add much to the quality of the sound." Holding up the violin he had used, he tossed it to a boy sitting on the front row. "Tonight I decided to leave my Stradivari at home," he called out. "Take that as a gift. It is quite inexpensive. But with practice you will find that it too can produce lovely music." The audience, aware of the circulating gossip, loved the gesture and roared its approval.

Whether this story be fact or fiction, it illustrates a great truth. Beauty can be produced from the most unpromising of instruments.

Part of the wonder of the gospel record is that Jesus used ordinary men and women to accomplish his purposes. This is both challenging and disturbing. Had Jesus required great scholarship and virtue before anyone could become a disciple, then poor frail mortals such as we would have been able to excuse ourselves. Had he chosen giants of faith, we could bemoan our lack of adequate personal resources. Jesus, however, chose the *ordinary*—fishermen, tax collectors, and even outcasts. As we travel with him and see him making disciples out of damaged and imperfect men and women, it is possible to catch a glimpse of what he may do with us when we are at his disposal. The wonder of the Christian story can be summarized with these words: "Second-rate instruments but first-rate music."

There is no more impressive example than that of Peter. No disciple is mentioned more often than he. Blustering, naive, stumbling, eager, wavering, failing, repenting, and weeping. Peter warms our hearts. He is lovable not in spite of his faults but *because* of them. As we see Jesus molding and mending him, we ought to be encouraged. Can the Master not do the same with we who are no less inadequate than Peter? As we journey with Jesus, a similar work of grace can take place in us.

Peter the perceptive

In Luke's Gospel we first meet Peter when Jesus used his boat as a pulpit. When the teaching session was over, Jesus told Peter, James, and John to let their nets down in deep water for a catch. Since they had been out fishing the preceding night and caught nothing, they were obviously tired. If they had failed at night, they were hardly likely to succeed during the less favorable conditions of daylight. Nevertheless, they reluctantly obeyed and were overwhelmed by an enormous catch. Peter was aware that something awesome had happened. His response was to fall on his knees and say, "Go away from me, Lord, for I am a sinful man!" (Luke 5:8).

Jesus is able to do much with someone who has this kind of awareness of personal inadequacy; with someone who has a sense of sin. A second-rate instrument, but capable of first-rate music.

Quite recently I preached at a most inspiring ecumenical gathering. I was a stranger to that particular city and was overwhelmed by the friendliness of the people. The church in which the rally was held was crowded, and the organizers were running out of space. A friend of mine who is never short of a choice word loves to say that few sounds are more encouraging to a congregation than the sound of extra chairs being brought in! A large choir provided special music. The congregational singing was thrilling, and there was a most receptive atmosphere for the preaching of the gospel.

As I stood at the door bidding farewell to some of the congregation at the end of the service, I was aware of a man hovering over to my right. He was about fifty years of age. He was obviously intent on having a word with me, but was waiting until the others had gone. Finally his patience was rewarded. The church officials were switching off the lights and collecting the hymn sheets as he approached me. I took his extended hand and he looked intently into my eyes. There was a haunting expression on his face. He thanked me for the address and then he added something which caused me to catch my breath. "Five years ago," he said, "I stood where you stand. It was not in this church or even in this city. Then I too, was a minister of the gospel and I had the church of my dreams. But I made some foolish decisions and I wandered away."

He paused. Choosing my words with care I said, "But there is always a way back when we are penitent." He took his hand out of mine and shook his head sadly. "There can be no way back for me," he said. And then he was gone. He almost ran down the steps of the church and out into the night. I went after him but when I reached the street he had disappeared into the November mist. I turned to two of the officials who were putting the hymn sheets away. "Who was that man?" I asked. "We don't know," they answered. "We have never seen him before."

His face haunts me still. You see, he was wrong. I wish there had been an opportunity to remind him of Peter and to affirm that there is always a way back when a person is aware of need and is prepared to repent. The instrument may be marred and, as a result, be considered second-rate. But in the hands of Jesus the music can still be the song of heaven. The glory of the gospel is of first-rate music produced from second-rate instruments.

Peter the passionate

Toward the end of his earthly journey, there is a tense moment when Jesus shares with his disciples his awareness of some of the anguish that lies ahead. "You will all become deserters because of me this night," he says (Matt. 26:31). Peter immediately replies, "Though all become deserters because of you, I will never desert you" (v. 33).

It is typical of Peter's passionate nature that he should rush in with such a ready denial without adequately counting the cost. Looking at the incident in the light of what followed, we are inclined to be dismissive of such a rash response; and in doing so, we are in danger of missing something quite vital. Peter's protestation was the product of a passionate nature. And Jesus welcomes passion because, when rightly channeled, the result can be exquisite.

Jacqueline du Pré, whose early death in 1987 at the age of forty-two plunged the world of music into mourning, is considered by many experts to be one of the greatest cellists of this century. Carol Easton, in her biography *Jacqueline du Pré: A Biography* (Hodder and Stoughton, 1989, p. 106), tells how just before her twenty-first birthday, Jacqueline du Pré played in Moscow at a concert with Rostropovich conducting. Afterward he told her, "Of all the cellists I've met of this generation, you are the most interesting. You can go the farthest—farther than me." Earlier, after her debut in Carnegie Hall, one critic had written, "Her performance stood the audience on its ravished ear." Her secret? Passion! She had a burning passion for the music of the cello, which manifested itself from a very early age. The cello was not just something that excited her interest or provided pleasure when she was in the mood for it. It *consumed* her; she utterly lost herself in it.

Translate this from the world of art to the world of faith. Passion can be sanctified. Under the deft and gentle hand of Christ, a passionate nature can be channeled into enthusiastic discipleship. It can make ordinary men and women into burning evangelists, so that they lose themselves in devotion to him. Indeed it is the *lack* of passion in discipleship that is most to be feared.

The great Scotsman Arthur J. Gossip wrote in *The Hero In Thy Soul* (Edinburgh: T & T Clark, 1929, p. 172) that scripture is clearly against the person who is half and half. "For the grossest sinner it has pity; for the clumsiest fumbler it has hope; even for Judas it has a strange almost eerie self-restrained and determined silence; but for a nameless thing that is nothing at all it feels only a horrible sick nausea and an instinctive shuddering of soul it cannot master." One of the most devastating criticisms made about any church is addressed to the church at Laodicea. "Because you are lukewarm, and neither cold nor hot, I am about to spit you out of my mouth" (Rev. 3:16).

There was nothing lukewarm about Peter. He brought his passionate nature and laid it at the feet of Christ. Yes, he may have made rash promises, but his heart was in the right place. And Jesus is able to do great things with such a person.

Of course, discipleship in our complicated age requires a cool head and a mind ready to respond to the best in modern scholarship. But there must also be a warm heart. True religion requires passion. Without it, the Christian faith is cold and lifeless. One of the most quoted sayings by an English churchman in this century is that of Dean Inge, who said, "Christianity is caught not taught." Of course he was right. And this holy contagion comes from hearts blazing with love of Christ. A consuming passion for God is the secret of effective discipleship. When that is present, though the instrument be second-rate, the music can be exquisite.

Peter the pardoned

The last recorded conversation that Jesus had with Peter was by the lakeside after the Resurrection. Peter had stumbled. He had denied his Lord and had broken down in tears of shame. For many, such an eclipse would have meant the end of the relationship with Christ. But thanks to the fisherman's penitent spirit, Jesus was able to take that damaged disciple and mend him through the wonder of pardon. "Simon son of John, do you love me?" he asked. Peter, passionate to the end, blurted out, "Lord, you know everything; you know that I love you." Jesus tenderly completed the work of restoration by giving him the task of a lifetime. "Feed my sheep" (John 21:15-17).

Although Peter had failed, he was not a failure. He was not like Judas, for whom the end was utter despair and finally self-destruction. And Peter learned much from the gentle handling he received from Jesus. Years later, when he was carrying out the commission he had received by the lakeside and was feeding the sheep, he sent a message to Christians undergoing terrible persecution at the hands of the Roman emperor Nero. His concluding words before his final greeting were, "And after you have suffered for a little while, the God of all grace, who has called you to his eternal glory in Christ, will himself restore, support, strengthen, and establish you" (1 Pet. 5:10).

The word Peter used for "restore" has about it the atmosphere of Galilee, where his journey with Jesus began. It is the same word used by Mark when he referred to James and John "mending the nets" (Mark 1:19). Right to the end of the pilgrimage, Peter could not forget that the Savior he served was one who took broken men and women and made them into disciples. Jesus was the mender who could take a second-rate instrument and from it bring forth first-rate music.

In the town where I grew up there was a remarkable pharmacist. Because of an illness he suffered during his youth, he was physically disabled. But through his damaged body a radiant spirit shone. There was something about him that was nothing less than sublime. He was loved by the entire community. Churches of all denominations welcomed him into their pulpits. Across the counter of his drugstore he dispensed compassion, wisdom, and spiritual guidance. His appearances as the visiting preacher at my home church were always memorable occasions. I used to hear the older members say lovingly of him, "The gospel is very powerful when it is preached from a pulpit of pain."

In one of his sermons, he told how one dark, wet night he heard a knock at the front door. He found there a small boy who obviously had fallen in the rain. He looked a pathetic sight; his knees were bleeding, and there was mud all down his jacket and across his face. With a sob the boy said, "Mr. Lightfoot, will you mend me?" Instinctively the child had come to the door of one who he knew was a "mender." It could be said of that good man that he spent his lifetime mending others, physically and spiritually. And this, as he so often testified, was because he himself had been mended by Christ.

Christ the mender is still at work. He is still taking second-rate instruments and from them producing the first-rate music of heaven. And he is not going to be defeated by second-rate instruments such as we.

But first we must be ready to travel with him.

Study Questions

1. Read Isaiah 6:1-8. The prophet's call arises out of his awareness of the need of his people (note v. 8). List some of the needs of which you are aware in the church and the community. Does this awareness of needs around you constitute a call for you? What are your plans for doing something about it? What is holding you back?

2. Read Jeremiah 18:1-6. The image of the potter is used to describe God reshaping that which is marred. But for this to be possible, the clay must be sufficiently pliable. How can we ensure that our lives do not become hard and brittle but remain sensitive to the molding hand of God? What role do worship, Bible study, and private prayer play in your life? What new ways of opening yourself to God might you try this Lent?

3. Read Matthew 14:22-33. What does this passage tell you about Peter and the way in which Jesus handles second-rate instruments? How can you apply it to your discipleship this Lent?

4. Name one or two outstanding experiences in your life of God "mending" you. Have you ever shared these with another person? How have these experiences affected the quality of your life? How is God producing first-rate music out of you?

Focus for the Week: Responding to Christ's Call

As you journey with Jesus through Lent, are you sufficiently perceptive to hear the call to become disciples? Have you heard the call but are reluctant to accept the challenge because you feel inadequate, aware that you are only a second-rate instrument? Or have you heard the call but are unwilling to make the changes in your life that you know will be necessary if God is going to use you? Are you prepared to offer what little you have to God and trust the Holy Spirit to produce first-rate music in your life?

The Third Week in Lent
Doing the Best Things at the Worst Times
(Accepting the Challenge)

> *If any want to become my followers, let them deny themselves and take up their cross and follow me. (Mark 8:34)*

Sometimes quite delightful experiences happen by chance. Several years ago when traveling toward the city of Nottingham, my wife, Brenda, and I saw a road sign to "Staunton Harold." That name stirred the embers of my memory. Hadn't I read somewhere that it was the name of an old manor with an interesting history? Unable to resist the impulse, we turned off the road to pay it a visit.

The manor is a stately house standing beside a lake and surrounded by meadows. Today it is the property of a well-known charity and provides a home for invalids who are able to enjoy the lovely surroundings. More than three centuries ago, during a turbulent period in English history, a member of the noble family who then owned the estate built the small, graceful church that stands just a few yards from the house. There is an inscription on the stone arch above the church door. It reads:

> In the year 1653 when all things sacred throughout the nation were either demolished or profaned, Sir Robert Shirley founded this church; whose singular praise it is to have done the best things at the worst times.

That last phrase is arresting. It is one thing to do noble things when all is going well, but to do the best things at the worst times requires special qualities. And this is the challenge that Jesus presents to anyone who wants to be a disciple.

These are difficult times for living the life of faith. Ours is a materialistic age. Worse, it is a time of moral relativity. Some things that once were regarded as either right or wrong are now considered to be matters of individual choice. Added to this are the perplexing ethical issues created by advancing knowledge. Technology appears to be outstripping moral philosophy. Because of the triumphs of medical science, for example, dramatic interventions are now possible at the early stages of life—with the unborn and the newborn—and also at life's closing chapter, with terminally ill persons whose lives can be artificially prolonged. New skills in genetic engineering offer brave vistas of a better life, and also fears of unspeakable terrors. Herein are moral minefields for persons of faith. "Let's get back to the simple gospel," our hearts whisper. If only the issues that the gospel is called to address were still so simple!

But before we throw up our hands in despair we should ask the question, "Is our generation unique? Are we the only ones who have had problems?" Of course not! Glance back to those first disciples who faced the tyranny of Rome, the hostility of their fellow countrymen, and the perilous uncertainty of leaving their livelihood. Or think of those brave men and women who confessed Christ right under the nose of Nero, that cruel and heartless persecutor of the church. Saints in Caesar's household! They would receive no certificate of appreciation or glowing citation for their faithfulness. But they did the best things at the worst times, and because of them the faith was kept glowing during dark, bleak days.

As we travel through Lent with Jesus, we find ourselves being challenged as were those first disciples. The Master does not come with easy promises of a comfortable journey. His words are stark and daunting: "If any want to become my followers, let them deny themselves and take up their cross and follow me" (Mark 8:34). But this challenge can also be seen as an exciting invitation to all that is highest and best within us, an appeal to nobility in our nature. It is a call to rise above our circumstances and do the best things at the worst times.

What does the acceptance of this challenge and invitation require as we travel with Jesus?

Accepting the challenge means being absolutely committed to Christ.

Whenever I am a little low in spirit, few things cheer me up as much as watching the video of the film *Chariots of Fire*. My heart kindles toward Eric Liddell, the devout Scottish Christian and Olympic champion who eventually died in World War II as a prisoner of war in the Far East. Because of his convictions, he was ready to forfeit an Olympic medal rather than run on a Sunday.

When his Olympic career was just dawning, Eric was helping at a Scottish Christian mission with his sister Jennie. She became anxious because of the growing interest of her brother in running. Was it going to eclipse his call to the mission field? There is a significant moment in the film when Eric and Jennie are on the hillside overlooking the city. "I've decided," Eric says to her, "I'm going back to China. The Missionary Society has accepted me." Jennie hugs him with delight. Then he detaches himself and adds, "But I've got a lot of running to do first. You've got to understand. I believe that God made me for a purpose, for China. He also made me *fast*. And when I run, I feel his pleasure. To give it up would be to hold him in contempt."

Whenever I see the film of Eric Liddell breasting the tape, arms wildly flailing the air, to win the Olympic gold, I want to cheer. I don't think many would say there was anything particularly graceful about his running. His was the wild unconventional gait of the naturally swift. God had indeed made him fast.

And yet he did have grace, a beautiful winsome grace of spirit. He went on to do the best things at the worst times. His commitment to Christ was complete. It was not just an Olympic medal that he was ready to lose rather than compromise his principles. Before he had completed his journey with Jesus, he proved ready to lose far more. He put behind him athletic glory and went to China and eventually to an untimely death.

Eric Liddell reminds us that commitment involves the whole of life. There is a robust healthiness in his recognition that he could glorify God as much on the running track as in the prayer meeting. There was no artificial division in his life between the sacred and the secular. Christ had the whole of him. He was utterly committed. And it is that kind of commitment that makes it possible for those who journey with Jesus to do the best things at the worst times.

Accepting the challenge means being resolutely obedient to Christ.

As newlyweds, our first home was in London, close to the river Thames. One day I commented on the abundance of brooms and brushes we had accumulated in so short a time. I counted at least two soft-bristled sweeping brooms, two tough yard-brooms, and hand brushes of all sizes. Since we were operating on a tight budget and neither my young bride nor I were very experienced with housekeeping, I gently suggested that, perhaps, we were being a little overenthusiastic in our support of the broom industry.

"It's all that Clean-Eazy salesman's fault," my wife, Brenda, explained. "He calls every three months. He is so nice and pleasant. He tells me he has a large family to support, and I just don't have the heart to refuse to buy something." "Leave him to me," I replied in a commanding manner. "The next time he calls, let me know. I will deal with him." Brenda was delighted. "But," she added in a cautionary tone, "I don't think you'll find it as easy as you imagine."

Four weeks later I was in my study when my wife came in. There was unmistakable mischievous glee on her face. "He's here," she announced. "Who?" I asked. "Why, the Clean-Eazy man of course," she replied. "I saw him coming up the drive. He'll be ringing the bell at any moment."

Even as she spoke, the bell rang. Donning my sternest look I went to the door. "This will only take a moment," I said. I was gone ten minutes. When I eventually returned—dare I confess it—there was yet another broom in my hand!

Brenda thought it was hilarious. Vainly I tried to explain, to her amused delight, that it was a very special broom. It could do all kinds of wonderful things because the nice Clean-Eazy man said so. I fear she was not convinced. I was reluctant to admit that she was right after all. I just wasn't tough enough to say No to that persuasive salesman.

In discipleship, obedience to Christ means that it is frequently necessary to say No with clear, uncompromising resolution. Many situations are not as innocent as that salesman at the front door. Some have far-reaching and lasting consequences that can cause moral shipwreck. They appear with siren voices and are quite beguiling. The writer of the book of Hebrews warns against these tempting dangers. In his illuminating and thought-provoking phrase, J. B. Phillips draws out the forcefulness of Hebrews 3:13. "Beware that none of you becomes *deaf and blind to God* through the delusive glamour of sin" (emphasis mine). The author of Hebrews is warning us that evil does not appear as the hideous thing it really is but as something very desirable. It has a terrible seductive power.

Deaf and blind to God—indifferent to God's love in Christ—that is the terrible result of losing resolve and being seduced into striking a compromise with evil.

G. A. Studdert Kennedy was perhaps the most well-known British chaplain of the First World War. He was also a poet. His most quoted work, entitled "Indifference," is compellingly relevant to the spirit of our age:

> When Jesus came to Golgotha they hanged Him on a tree,
> They drave great nails through hands and feet, and made a Calvary;
> They crowned Him with a crown of thorns, red were His wounds and deep,
> For those were crude and cruel days, and human flesh was cheap.
>
> When Jesus came to Birmingham, they simply passed Him by,
> They never hurt a hair of Him, they only let Him die;

> For men had grown more tender, and they would not give Him pain,
> They only just passed down the street, and left Him in the rain.
>
> Still Jesus cried, "Forgive them, for they know not what they do,"
> And still it rained the wintry rain that drenched Him through and through;
> The crowds went home and left the streets without a soul to see,
> And Jesus crouched against a wall and cried for Calvary.
> (*The Unutterable Beauty,* New York: Harper & Brothers, 1936, p. 24)

If we would do the best things at the worst times we must be sensitive to the delusive glamour of sin and resolute in our rejection of any compromise in our discipleship.

Accepting the challenge means being a channel for the love of God.

A short time ago the news that a certain woman had died revived a very precious memory of my early days in medical practice. I remembered the first time I met her. She was then middle-aged and looking after her elderly father, who had been a widower for many years. She was a kind and happy person who had given up her post as a schoolteacher some years earlier in order to care for her ailing parents. She had nursed her mother through a long debilitating terminal illness and was then doing the same for her father.

It was my custom to make a house call at least once a month to see the patient. It would have been gratifying and comforting to discover that the warm-hearted sacrificial devotion of this remarkable woman was appreciated by her fortunate father. It was not! Far from being grateful, the old man was abusive and rude. He made unreasonable demands upon her. He became angry if she left the house for any length of time and was even resentful because she regularly attended church. I assumed at first that he was querulous because he was nervous about his declining strength. I then discovered that he had been equally unpleasant for years and had made life miserable first for his wife and then for his daughter.

On one of my regular visits shortly before his death, I found her washing him. After she had finished I carried out my examination and then wrote the necessary prescription. As I wrote, I pointed to the Bible on the table and raised the subject of faith with the old man, hoping that an opportunity might arise for me to slip in a word of Christian witness. My words had the opposite effect. They caused him to launch into a tirade of abuse against the church and all who supported it. He denounced all Christians as hypocrites and, pointing to his daughter, said that she was one of the worst of them. He went on to ridicule her faith and her waste of time supporting the church. I glanced at the daughter. I could see that there was no resentment or hostility, only pity and love in her eyes. She said nothing in reply but just quietly took away the bowl and the towel and made him comfortable once more. I have to confess that I lacked her grace. I was seething with indignation at such outrageous ingratitude and had difficulty not uttering a few home truths.

As we left the bitter old man on his couch and walked down the corridor to the front door, I tried to offer a word of encouragement. I told her how much I admired her skillful and devoted care. I added that I realized her task was all the harder because she was so unappreciated. She smiled and, without the slightest self-pity, said these words, which came immediately to my mind when I heard of her death: "Please don't worry about me, doctor. I don't mind. You see, I am doing this for God."

When a person becomes a channel for the love of God, the best things can be done in the worst times. And this is the challenge that Jesus presents as we journey with him.

More than thirty years ago I was walking down a city street in the North of England when I was stopped in my tracks by a pathetic sight. Across the road a blind man had been feeling his way by tapping his white cane against the wall. He had come to a point where builders were working and part of the wall had been demolished. He was standing there looking bewildered, his cane flailing the air. I went across and asked if I could be of assistance. "Why, yes," he said. "I usually follow the wall and it turns the corner. But something seems to be wrong," and he pointed with his cane to the place where the wall had stood. I explained. "They are rebuilding. That part of the wall has been demolished." The man turned his sightless eyes to me. "Then I am lost," he said. "Can you help me to get to Deansgate?"

We live in an age when familiar landmarks are disappearing; the landmarks of morality, family values, honesty, and integrity. Jesus challenges us to a journey of discipleship that will help to restore them. He calls us to do the best things at the worst times. Have we the courage to make this journey?

Study Questions

1. Read Daniel 3:13-18 and Acts 4:18-31. Most of us have met or heard of men and women with the kind of faith that does not consider personal safety or advantage when obeying the challenge of Christ—such as Christians who remained faithful in Nazi-dominated Germany. Do you believe such courage is natural or acquired? why? On your Lenten journey, how can you cultivate this kind of selfless devotion?

2. To accept the challenge of Jesus means that we must honor him in all of our life and not just in part. Is there any part of your life or occupation in which Jesus cannot be honored? Can anything be done about it?

3. What would be your advice to someone who was the object of verbal or physical abuse either at work or at home? Is it always possible to do the best things at the worst times? How can we help one another to cope with failure when we find that we are just unable to go on loving and caring? Think of a time when you felt unable to go on loving. What did you do?

4. What are the moral and spiritual landmarks that you feel are missing in our world today and what do you think can be done to restore them?

Focus for the Week: Responding to Christ's Challenge

To accept the challenge of Christ and attempt to do the best things at the worst times is anything but easy. As we journey toward the Cross and discover the cost of loving and giving, we realize how difficult it really is.

Do you have the courage to say "yes" to the things that ennoble and "no" to those that degrade, even when this affects your popularity or your material success? Are you willing to be as a light in the world? (Matt. 5:14-16).

The Fourth Week in Lent
Reflections of Jesus (Being Healed)

A leper came to him begging him, and kneeling he said to him, "If you choose, you can make me clean." Moved with pity, Jesus stretched out his hand and touched him, and said to him, "I do choose. Be made clean!" (Mark 1:40-41)

Some years ago I was clearing out a box of newspaper clippings that had been left in the garage for a long time. They had become damp and moldy, but nevertheless, parting with them was like parting with old friends.

One clipping that had to be discarded had been sent to me by an elderly correspondent. It was a newspaper photograph taken during a visit of the late King George VI to a dockyard in the North of England shortly before the outbreak of World War II. The picture was of a boy about nine or ten years of age. Evidently he had come with his father's lunch. The last thing his mother expected when she sent him on his errand was that he would have a royal audience. He was photographed looking disheveled with his cap askew. The king was bending down to speak to him. Although only the side of the monarch was visible, it was obvious that the look on the face of the king was one of kindness as he spoke to the child: It was reflected in the boy's bright sparkling eyes and broad grin.

Most of us have seen Jesus reflected in the lives of the Christian men and women who have influenced us. Likewise, when we turn to the gospel story and journey with Jesus there, we see his reflection in those who were transformed by his influence. Nowhere is this more visible than when he does the unthinkable by reaching out and touching a man with leprosy, a man whom nobody wanted. And in touching, Jesus brings wholeness. In the man with leprosy, we see the reflection of Christ the healer.

Christ the healer restores our humanity.

In the second half of the film version of Pierre Boulle's novel *The Bridge over the River Kwai*, there is a memorable scene. A small select team has been dispatched by the Allied High Command to destroy the bridge constructed by prisoners of war across the River Kwai. The team's journey takes them through occupied territory, and they stumble into an enemy patrol. It is essential that the members of the group conceal their presence from the Japanese so that they will not be expected when they reach the bridge.

Suddenly the youngest member of the Allied group comes face to face with a Japanese soldier. He is aware that this member of the enemy patrol must not be allowed to escape and report the presence of his special detachment. He knows that there is only one course of action for him to take if the element of surprise, which is essential to the mission, is to be preserved. For a few moments the two young men stand looking at each other, both of them rooted to the spot. Just then all the young soldier's training for his special mission deserts him. His instructors had taught him how to kill "the enemy" silently. But this Japanese soldier standing there looking at him is not the impersonal "enemy" about which he had been taught. He is just another young man like himself. This Japanese youth is a person. He has a face. He looks bewildered and scared. He too is a long way from home and loved ones. And, because the young Allied soldier sees his foe as a person, not the anonymous "enemy," he cannot bring himself to attack and kill.

We are able to do terrible things to people once we depersonalize them. Once we label them, it is so much easier to forget that they have hearts, minds, dreams, and feelings, just like us.

It is significant that this man who came to Jesus for healing is given no name in Mark's account. It was probably not known. He is just referred to as a leper. He was a problem, a social outcast. He had been labeled and then discarded. And this is not an isolated case recorded in the New Testament.

When Jesus is invited to a meal in the house of Simon the Pharisee, Luke tells us that the normal courtesies of a considerate host were ignored (Luke 7:36-50). Then something dramatic happens. A woman who was socially unacceptable slips in and kneels at the feet of Jesus as the Master reclines at dinner. She weeps over his feet and anoints them with perfume. The host seethes with indignation. "If this man were a prophet, he would have known who and what kind of woman this is who is touching him—that she is a sinner." Labeled! For Simon the Pharisee, there is nothing more to be said. Her personhood is tossed away. But Jesus sees beyond the label. He sees her as a child of God. His tender treatment of her contrasts sharply with that of the Pharisee. Jesus recognizes her inherent worth in her capacity to love, and in offering her a new beginning he confers upon her the dignity that Simon and his label would have taken away.

Leslie Weatherhead, in his book *The Transforming Friendship* (London: Epworth Press, 1935, p. 112), tells of the census taker who called at one house to find out who lived there. He asked the woman who opened the door what children she had. She said, "Well, there's Willie and 'Orace and Ethel—" The census taker interrupted. "Never mind names; I just want numbers." Indignantly the woman replied, "In this house they haven't got numbers; every one of them has a name."

To the Master, the man imploring him for help was not "a leper," a problem; he was a human being *who happened to have leprosy.* That is a very different thing. And as he rises from his knees he is ennobled. His humanity has been restored and his personal worth has been affirmed. We see reflected in him the face of Christ the healer, who treats each of us as a unique individual precious to God.

Christ the healer restores our hope.

Out of the tens of thousands of survivors of the concentration camps of World War II, I have met just one. She was a middle-aged lady full of courage and laughter. She bubbled with vitality as she talked about her children and her grandchildren. I had guessed from her name and her accent that she was not English, but she did not say anything about her haunting background. I had no idea what she had been through. It came as a shock when I examined her to find on her arm that there was a number tattooed. She could see that I had noticed it, and as our eyes met, she nodded. "Yes, it is what you think it is, Doctor. It is my little war souvenir."

Later she talked about it. She told me of the Allied airman who took refuge in her parents' barn after his plane had been shot down and how her family sheltered him until he made contact with the underground and was guided back to England. "That was how we came to join the Resistance," she explained. "We were not particularly brave. We just drifted into it. It was something we thought had to be done. We lived in hope that the invasion would come before very long and then we could return to our normal routine. But the war had dragged on and finally our resistance group was discovered."

Then she told me how one by one the precious things in her life were taken away. First the secret police came and arrested her parents. Then her brother was captured. Finally she, herself, was put on a train and taken to the camp where her little keepsakes such as a few photographs of her family and a locket with her mother's picture in it were taken away. "But the worst thing of all," she said, "was when they put that number on my arm. It is awful when someone takes your name away. It seems the bitter end. That was when I lost hope."

"Then," she added, "they made me work in the sewing room where I met a marvelous woman. She was a devout Christian. We were not supposed to talk but she used to whisper words of comfort. One text she used to say every day: 'We do not grieve as those who have no hope.' It was because of her that I too became a Christian. I decided that I was not going to allow a barbarous regime to rob me of hope." She laughed and added, "And so you see, I survived."

Not all have the inner resources of that remarkable woman. There are experiences that can rob us of our hope such as the loss of loved ones, desertion by family members or friends, physical and verbal abuse, and, of course, disease.

As a physician, I have seen firsthand the despair caused by slowly progressive disorders that gradually sap physical powers. I have watched sufferers struggle bravely as each day another skill or ability slips away. I have seen how their hearts almost break because of the sense of uselessness that overwhelms them. The ebbing away of self-esteem is, perhaps, the most terrible part of the condition. The patient begins to feel a burden to others, especially to family and friends. Gradually interest in life is lost, and each day becomes just another twenty-four hours to be endured.

There also are many who suffer from invisible hurts. Outwardly they look well enough, putting on a brave face in public. But in private, they wrestle with debilitating illnesses of the mind. Perhaps they struggle with depression, which takes them into a dark abyss day after day. Or perhaps they struggle with anxiety sometimes associated with prostrating panic attacks. Their friends mean well when they say, "Just pull yourself together and make an effort to snap out of it!" If only it were so simple. For these sufferers, just getting through the day is an act of incredible heroism.

This man with leprosy represents sufferers everywhere. He knew how a loss of self-esteem together with a heavy sense of helplessness could take away all hope. Once, no doubt, he had lived among family. Once he had participated in the community, joining with his neighbors in the joys of weddings and birthdays and in the fellowship of worship. But then the disease had struck.

At first, perhaps, he hid it, not telling anyone about his loss of sensation, often a first symptom. But once the physical effects began to appear, everyone was aware. No one wanted to know him. He was shunned because he was seen as a threat; he could contaminate. He had to leave home, family, and neighbors, because he was commanded by the law to keep a distance from the rest of society. The only way he could survive was through charity. He had to become a beggar! It is not difficult to imagine how a growing sense of hopelessness overwhelmed him.

And then one day, greatly daring, he approached Jesus. It was the desperate gesture of one who was willing to defy the law. He did not keep his distance. He came up close. "If you choose, you can make me clean," he cried. There was only one response possible for one as sensitive as the Master. "Jesus stretched out his hand and touched him, and said to him, 'I do choose. Be made clean!' " (Mark 1:41).

I see light dawning again in this man's eyes. I see hope replacing despair. I see him rising from his knees, looking Jesus in the eyes, and feeling a reason for living once more. He is a transformed person. And in this restored leper I see a reflection of Christ the healer.

Christ the healer assures us that we are children of God.

One Christmas, the surgeon Paul Brand delivered a sermon that has traveled far beyond its origin in the Vellore Christian Hospital Community in India, where he had done so much in repairing the ravages of leprosy. It was delivered, almost by chance, in the courtyard of a house near the hospital. It was an informal gathering. The "congregation" consisted mainly of men and women who suffered from the disease.

A Christmas party was in progress. Dr. Brand had slipped in after a hard day's work. The address he gave was impromptu as he responded to the pleas of those present for him to say a few words. In her book *Ten Fingers for God* (Hodder and Stoughton, 1966, pp. 156f.), Dorothy Clarke Wilson tells the story: "Paul felt empty of ideas. But he knew he must think of something. As he rose to his feet he became suddenly conscious of hands, dozens of them, many raised palm to palm in the familiar gesture of *Namaste,* some arched in the shape of claws, some with all five fingers, some with no fingers, some with a few stumps, some half hidden to cover their disfigurement."

Wilson then describes how the words of the surgeon were translated into Tamil and Hindi. Paul Brand said:

> I am a hand surgeon so when I meet people I can't help looking at their hands. The palmist claims he can tell your future by looking at your hands. I can tell your past. For instance, I can tell what your trade has been by the position of the calluses and the condition of the nails. I can tell a lot about your character. I love hands.
>
> He went on to talk about the hands of Jesus as he traced the Master's ministry. Finally he said:
>
> Then there were his crucified hands. It hurts me to think of a nail being driven through the center of any hand, because I know what goes on there, the tremendous complex of tendons and nerves and blood vessels and muscles. It is impossible to drive a spike through its center without crippling it. The thought of those healing hands being crippled reminds me of what Christ was prepared to endure. In that act he identified himself with all the deformed and crippled human beings in the world. Not only was he able to endure poverty with the poor, weariness with the tired, but—*clawed hands with those crippled.*

As he finished, Paul was again conscious of hands as all over the courtyard they were lifted, palm to palm, with the same stumps or lack of fingers, the same scars, the same crooked arches. Yet not the same. No one tried to hide them. They were held higher, close to the face, almost with pride. Even the stumps seemed to have acquired a certain dignity.

As I think of the thousands who have been given hope through the dedicated hands of this great surgeon and Christian, I see reflected in those men and women the face of Christ the healer.

We all hurt. Some of our hurts are, perhaps, emotional, stemming from abuse we may have received in the past from others. Some are the result of a loss of self-esteem through either mental or physical illness. As we journey through Lent, we encounter Jesus the healer, reflected through lives that have been touched and changed by the wholeness he confers. We too, can experience this wholeness that comes from One who identified with our condition and who comes to us in our need assuring us that we are children of God.

Study Questions

1. In what ways are men and women today denied their basic human rights? Are we as individual Christians and collectively as churches active enough in seeking to promote human dignity? Can you think of any active measure you could take or recommend to your community or church?

2. Is there someone you know who needs his or her self-esteem restored? How can you make a point this week to allow Jesus to reach out through you to that person?

3. Does the church today have a specific ministry of physical healing or is its task that of supporting the medical profession and patients with encouragement and prayer? What role are you to play in this?

4. Read Luke 17:11-19, the story of the ten lepers. Jesus said to the man who returned to thank him, "Get up and go on your way; your faith has made you well" (v. 19). Knowing that the other nine ungrateful ones had also been healed, what do you think was the significance of these words addressed to the one who expressed gratitude? Was there something different in his healing? If so, what do you think it was?

Focus for the Week: Wholeness in Christ

By the way in which he treated men and women, Jesus has shown us that health is not just a physical experience but involves also the healing of mind, emotions, and spirit. Do we reflect this awareness of the needs of others by the way in which we treat them?

At the end of each day this week, reflect on the way in which your words and actions have reflected Jesus and the ways you have acted as an instrument in his continuing healing ministry.

The Fifth Week in Lent
The Mountain and the Valley (Gathering Strength)

Peter said to Jesus, "Rabbi, it is good for us to be here; let us make three dwellings, one for you, one for Moses, and one for Elijah. He did not know what to say, for they were terrified." (Mark 9:5-6)

Once I presided at a large ecumenical service that marked the culmination of weeks of prayer and preparation. The organizers were delighted with the attendance. The lovely historic church was packed to the door with people from all denominations, many of whom had traveled considerable distances.

The preacher, an old friend of mine, was well known. He had exercised a distinguished ministry both as a teacher and a writer. I had prepared my introduction with care. I had promised him that I would be brief, but I was anxious to do justice to his impressive record. Having completed my remarks, I sat down as my friend rose. There was a pause of several seconds, which seemed like an eternity, as hundreds of faces turned expectantly toward him. When the service was over, after he had thrilled us with his moving address, we enjoyed a chuckle over that tense beginning. He told me that as he rose to his feet, his mind suddenly went blank. He had finally pulled himself together, but his opening words came out in the wrong order. He began, "Thank you for your generous introduction. I don't appreciate what you have said, but I deserve it from the bottom of my heart."

It is comforting to know that even the most experienced speakers can be tongue-tied. We all know what it is like. We know what we want to say, but the words refuse to come in their proper order. In his Gospel, Mark tells us that Peter was in this state when Jesus was transfigured before him on the mountain.

Meanwhile, something was happening in the valley where the rest of the disciples waited. A deeply distressed man had brought his epileptic son to be cured. The disciples had tried to help but had been unable to heal him.

Here is a study in contrasts. On the mountain, Jesus and three of his disciples are experiencing a high and holy moment. Down in the valley, an unfortunate boy is convulsed while his father and the disciples look on helplessly. The two scenes belong together.

There is a famous painting of the Transfiguration by the Renaissance artist Raphael. In it Jesus is talking to Moses and Elijah on the mountaintop. At first glance it appears as though this sensitive artist has uncharacteristically spoiled the effect by including in the same picture the distressing events in the valley. The artist portrays the father pointing urgently up the mountain to Jesus who is wrapped in heavenly communion.

Clearly Raphael's picture is geographically absurd. The distance between the two scenes was far too great for them to be included sensibly on the same canvas. But Raphael has not blundered. With unerring insight he has seen that the rapture of the mountain and the tragedy of the valley are parts of a whole.

As we journey with Jesus through Lent, we see that our discipleship lies in that creative tension between the mountain and the valley. Without the worship on the mountain, there is no inspiration for Christian service. Without service in the valley, worship is incomplete.

The mountain provides insight.

I once led a clergy retreat at a farm that is also a Franciscan Friary. We were guests of the Franciscan Brothers; our meetings were held in the Refectory. The fellowship with the clergy and the Brothers was warm and uplifting. The Franciscans fascinated me. They worked the farm, tending cattle, pigs, sheep, and chickens. They tilled fields and vegetable gardens. They cared for fruit trees. Their beehives produced honey. At midday all work temporarily ceased. A bell tolled above the chapel, which was a converted cowshed, calling the community to Holy Communion.

We visitors interrupted our sessions to join in this act of worship. Glancing around the chapel, I was struck by the significance of what was happening. As the Franciscans paused and celebrated Holy Communion, they were making a profound statement. They were saying that all their activity was to be viewed from the standpoint of worship; that their lives could not be measured in terms of livestock, cereals, vegetables, honey, or fruit. They could be understood only in terms of the kingdom of God to which there was access through the life, death, and resurrection of Jesus Christ. In their worship— their mountaintop—the Franciscans gained insight into who they were and affirmed that they were not made for the farm; they were made for God.

The fundamental questions about human nature are neither asked nor answered in the valley.

The kind of questions that are asked in the valley are about how much we earn, how large our houses are, and what sort of cars we drive. The valley measures us in terms of anatomy and biology, education and social position, power and influence. But these dimensions are quite inadequate for the measurement of life or the facing of death. On the mountain, however, everything is measured on a grander scale. There we are reminded that we come from God and that we shall return to God; that we are made in the divine image and likeness, and that our lives have meaning only when seen within the economy of God. Augustine speaks for all those who would journey with Jesus: "Thou hast made us for Thyself and our hearts are restless until they find their rest in Thee."

The mountain provides direction.

The mountain is the place of vision. The valley is the place of obedience. Once I was being taken by car toward the western border of North Carolina. We reached a point in the road where my host said, "We are now crossing the Eastern Watershed. Up to this point, all the rain that falls flows into the Atlantic Ocean. Beyond this point it flows into the Mississippi River."

It is significant that Simon Peter's confession to Jesus, "You are the Messiah" (Mark 8:29), immediately precedes the account of the Transfiguration. Here we reach a watershed in the ministry of Jesus. Prior to this time he has seldom referred to his coming suffering and death. From this time on, as Jesus turns toward Jerusalem, this becomes the dominant theme. The cross is now clearly in view. With the vision had come direction. Jesus would not falter. He would drink the cup that had been given to him.

For Paul, the mountain was the road to Damascus where he met the risen Jesus. His valley was the grim world of prison, rejection, and eventual death. "But," he said, "I was not disobedient to the heavenly vision."

During our Lenten journey with Jesus, the mountain is our time of quiet private devotion each day, as well as those moments of corporate worship with God's people. There, if we have eyes to see and ears to hear, we are given direction for our life of service. The valley where we live out that vision is our community, our daily work, our family relationships, our encounters with friends and neighbors.

The valley is not always a happy or pretty place. Unfortunately the people we go to serve are not always pleasant and grateful. There are times when we may prefer to have nothing to do with them. The vision on the mountain, however, gives our lives their direction. We return to the valley as Christ's disciples. We serve humanity not for its own sake but for the sake of the Master.

The mountain provides strength.

The voices of the valley tell us to stir ourselves up and try harder. But the fires of compassion within us grow cold when people don't deserve it. We need to be inspired. We need a power beyond ourselves. The mountain is the place where such strength is given. The valley is the place where that strength is used.

For most of us there are moments when we question our faith. We have dry seasons in our pilgrimage when the skies are gray and overcast. There are moments when confidence ebbs and we begin to ask deep and uneasy questions. At such times we must trust our higher vision. We must trust the moments on the mountain.

Years ago I heard a preacher tell of a reluctant witness who was being cross-examined. The witness was being pressed very hard to admit that if a certain event had actually happened as he claimed, then it was nothing less than a miracle. Because the witness was a bricklayer, the lawyer used a bricklaying analogy.

"Let us suppose that you are going up a ladder with a hod of bricks on your shoulder," he said. "At the last rung from the top your foot slips and you fall to the ground. Happily you are not hurt. You get up and find that not a single brick has spilled out of the hod. What would you call that?" "I would call it remarkable," said the bricklayer.

"Very well," said the lawyer, trying to stay calm. "You get up. You pick up that remarkable hod. Once again you mount the ladder. On the last rung from the top your foot slips again. You fall to the ground. Happily once again you are not hurt. You get up and find that yet again not a single brick has spilled out of the hod. What would you call that?" "I would call it a coincidence," said the bricklayer.

"Very well," said the lawyer, controlling himself only with an effort. "Once again you climb that ladder with the hod on your shoulder. Yet again on the last rung from the top you slip. Yet again you fall to the ground. Happily once more you are not hurt. You get up and find that not a single brick has spilled out of the hod. What would you call that?" "I would call it a habit!" the witness replied.

It is sad that instead of being a miracle of inspiration on the mountain, worship easily becomes a habit. Sad? Oh much worse than sad for the life of the disciple. It is tragic. It is only through the miracle of the mountain that we find strength for service in the valley. On the mountain we have a vision, the high moment when we see who we are and what we are to do. But also with the vision we are given inner resources. Down in the valley we have our darkness and our doubts when those resources are desperately needed. It is only by the strength received with Jesus on the mountain that we can journey with him through the valley. When the darkness gathers and the doubts descend, we need that miracle of worship to sustain us.

Outstanding preacher Charles Haddon Spurgeon once told of a friend who went to live in a city in the northeast of England at the end of the nineteenth century, when the air of that city was filled with smoke from all the factories.

The newcomer was looking at a house that was available for rent. As he looked out of the window in the top room, the landlord said to him, "You can see Durham Cathedral from here on a Sunday." Spurgeon's friend asked, "Why on Sunday more than any other day?" "Well," replied the landlord, "the furnaces are not going, and the smoke is not rising to darken the atmosphere."

In worship on Sunday we can see much more than a mere cathedral. We can see the gates of heaven. But this is also true of worship at any time. It is true of the daily times of quiet we spend with God during Lent. We see beyond time to eternity. We see beyond the narrow confines of our lives to the heart of God. And that vision brings with it strength.

We are reaching the point in our Lenten journey when the cross is in sight. We need the strength of the mountain if we are to face the challenge of Calvary. Indeed, whenever in our journey with Jesus we come to the dark and lonely places of the spirit, we must hold fast to the vision that we received on the mountain. As a wise friend once said to me, *"It is foolish to doubt in the dark what God has told us in the light."*

Study Questions

1. Have you had any "mountaintop" experiences? List them and the ways in which they have influenced your journey with Jesus.

2. Do you think it would be possible for anyone who knew you well to make an adequate assessment and summary of your life without any reference to that part of you which belongs to Christ? What influence has your journey with Jesus made upon the important decisions that you have made in your life so far?

3. Read Acts 26:1-23. Many of us, if we are perfectly honest with ourselves, would have to confess that we know of times when we have been disobedient to the heavenly vision (see v. 19). What has been the main reason in your journey with Jesus for failing in obedience? Has it been lack of courage, lack of idealism, lack of moral integrity, or some other thing? What have you learned from your failure? What is now different in your spiritual life that would make it less likely for you to fail again?

4. How can we make sure that worship remains a miracle and doesn't descend into becoming just a habit? List some of the things that you can do and pray for that would help you to discover the miracle on Sunday morning.

Focus for the Week: Going to the Mountain

We have to spend time in the valley. That is where our duties lie. We don't *have* to spend time on the mountain, but we need to!

Has your life been dominated by the valley and have you at times lost sight of the mountain? On your Lenten journey, resolve that your visits to the mountain are going to be more frequent and that you are going to introduce its atmosphere in your home, your workplace, and your community.

The Sixth Week in Lent
The Cry of Human Need (Meditating on His Suffering)

When Jesus knew that all was now finished, he said . . . "I am thirsty." (John 19:28)

I preached my first sermon in a small village church. Although I had no previous experience and had not at that time been to seminary, an emergency had arisen and I was asked to assist. As I was familiar with the village, I carefully wrote down the detailed travel instructions given me. They did not make a great deal of sense, and I expressed bewilderment. "Don't worry," I was told. "It really isn't as difficult as it sounds. Just take the bus to the village. When you get off, you will see a winding lane. Go along that lane until you come to the cross. When you come to the cross, my instructions will become much clearer to you."

The cross that was referred to was an old stone cross, similar to those that stand at the heart of many old English towns and villages. As I have recalled those words across the years, I have seen in them a deeper significance that was not intended at the time.

Our Lenten journey has inevitably brought us to the cross. The triumphant shouts of "Hosanna! / Blessed is the one who comes in the name of the Lord!" (Mark 11:9), which rang out when Jesus entered Jerusalem at the beginning of Holy Week, were short-lived. By Friday, harsher voices filled the air with the cry, "Crucify!" Later three crosses were raised outside the city wall, and many assumed that the story of Jesus had ended.

They were wrong! For Christians, the cross of Calvary marked a beginning. The symbol of torture and death became transformed into one of healing and life. Since that time, when we have come to the cross with Easter eyes, that symbol of shame and agony has proclaimed a marvelous message that we on our Lenten journey need to hear afresh. As we meditate on our Savior's agony, it is possible to hear Jesus' cry, "I am thirsty" at three levels of understanding, each of which offers a window into the heart of God.

Jesus' cry came from the depths of humanity.

Some years ago, on a Friday in December, I was traveling with my family to London where I was to preach at the Central Hall, Westminster. We had a two-door car and, in a day when safety belts were seldom used, our two small children were playing on the rear seat. It was just after Christmas and all their presents were in the trunk—they had insisted on bringing them. Suddenly we hit a thick wall of fog, our car skidded on the icy road, and we became part of a multiple-car accident. We were hurled about the vehicle which, to our horror, then burst into flames.

Mercifully my door was undamaged. I scrambled out and helped my wife, Brenda, to the side of the road. I lifted the children out and carried them to her. Then, despite their entreaties, I went back to the blazing car to rescue their Christmas presents from the trunk just before the gasoline tank exploded. I handed the children to the paramedics when they arrived, and we were all taken to the hospital. Once there I again helped in carrying the children out of the ambulance and then assisted my wife into a wheelchair so that she could be taken into surgery. And then, when all my family were being cared for, I suddenly felt agonizing pain. It was several weeks before my fractured ribs healed. There are psychological and physiological reasons why until that moment my mind had refused to register pain.

The apostle John tells us that it was after Jesus had prayed for his enemies, reassured the dying malefactor, taken care of his mother, and experienced the full horror of spiritual separation from God, that he then addressed his own physical needs with the words "I am thirsty" (John 19:28). And in those words we are reminded that Jesus had become one with all the suffering of the world. Until that moment he had not shown any indication that he was in agony.

It was not unusual for crucified persons to speak on the cross; but their words were usually snarls of hostility aimed at those who had caused their suffering, pleas for mercy, cries of agony, or even railings against God. In marked contrast, however, the first word of Jesus was "Father, forgive them; for they do not know what they are doing" (Luke 23:34). Before such amazing love for those who wronged him, we are silent in wonder. Such is almost beyond our comprehension. Could such a one be wholly human?

In that cry "I am thirsty," however, we have an affirmation that Jesus truly suffered there upon the cross and that he was fully human. Yet faith goes one important step farther. It claims that the risen and exalted Savior continues to share the suffering of all humankind. His resurrection body still bears the marks of the nails. Our humanity and the suffering he experienced have become part of the nature of God.

The doctrine of the Incarnation affirms that Jesus became representative of all humanity. When men and women suffer pain, physical want, indignity, and shame, the cry "I thirst" comes once again from the heart of God. Here is a cry from the depths of the darkest human experience which, through his cross, Jesus shared. He experienced our pain and has taken it into the Godhead.

Jesus' cry was addressed to the depths of humanity.

Was this cry an appeal for help? I believe it was. It seems incredible that Jesus did not give up on human nature even when nailed to the cross. He still believed that out there, in all that bigotry and cruel hate, someone might hear and respond.

John tells us that in response to his cry, Jesus is offered a drink of wine (19:29-30). Matthew, in what is generally regarded as referring to the same incident, adds a significant detail: "At once one of them ran and got a sponge, filled it with sour wine, put it on a stick, and gave it to him to drink" (Matt. 27:48). Some unnamed soldier responded to his cry.

I had those soldiers all figured out. They were a callous and bestial lot. They could be excused for hammering nails into the hands of Jesus because that was what execution duty required. But did they have to play the buffoon and add ridicule to cruel torture? Did they have to put a purple robe on him, crush a crown of thorns on his head, and mockingly hail him as "King of the Jews" (John 19:1-3)? Yes, it is easy to put a label on them. They are cruel, heartless, cynical, and evil. And just when we have closed the chapter on them, we are told that one ran to bring Jesus a drink. He *ran!*

When I was a medical student, a group of us were gathered one morning in a large Victorian ward that housed about thirty patients. We were gathered around the bed of a patient. With that patient's permission, the professor was giving us a tutorial on the signs and symptoms of his particular illness.

At the far end of the ward a nurse entered, pushing a cart loaded with instruments. A member of our group was becoming very fond of her and, just then, they exchanged meaningful glances. This welcome distraction meant that she did not notice a large industrial floor polisher in her path. The cart struck it and instruments were sent flying in all directions, landing with a noisy clatter on the tiled floor. Our colleague immediately detached himself from the bedside and ran across the ward to help the distressed nurse. A thunderous voice bellowed his name and summoned him to return. Then, with a twinkle in his eye, the professor said to the crestfallen student, "There are only three reasons for running in this hospital. The first is fire, the second is cardiac arrest, the third is hemorrhage. I am unable to see any of those emergencies. Go and help the nurse if you wish. Take her out to dinner. Marry her. But walk!" He was a compliant student, and he did all three. But that day he walked.

Running implies urgency. When the prodigal son came home, Luke tells us that the father ran to meet him (Luke 15:20). When I read of this soldier running, I realize that never again must I write anyone off as being entirely evil. Never again must I despair of a change of heart. Never again must I consider that anyone is beyond the appeal of love.

> Down in the human heart, crushed by the tempter,
> Feelings lie buried that grace can restore.
> Touched by a loving hand, wakened by kindness,
> Chords that were broken will vibrate once more.
> (Fanny J. Crosby)

I wish I knew his name! This soldier is yet another in that gallery of nameless men and women who eased the way for the Savior. He takes his place with the nameless leper who returned to give thanks when the other nine did not give it a thought; with the woman who anointed the Savior's feet with her perfume; with the woman at the well who gave him a drink; with a boy who brought his lunch with which Jesus fed a multitude. I wish I knew the name of this soldier who stands out in the carnival of hate and offers mercy in the form of a drink.

But perhaps I do know his name. For a crucified Christ calls out, from a million broken, hungry, thirsty, dying men, women, and children across the world, "I thirst." Perhaps that soldier bears our name! Did not Jesus say, "I was thirsty and you gave me something to drink. . . . Just as you did it to one of the least of these who are members of my family, you did it to me" (Matt. 25:35-40)?

Jesus' cry was addressed to the heart of God.

The devotional writer J. Neville Ward sees a deeper significance in Jesus' words "I am thirsty." He points to the solemnity with which John introduces the cry. "After this, when Jesus knew that all was now finished, he said . . . 'I am thirsty.' " Ward believes that John intended a spiritual as well as a physical dimension. Jesus had referred to his coming ordeal as "a cup." When Peter tried to defend him with a sword, Jesus had said, "Put your sword back into its sheath. Am I not to drink the cup that the Father has given me?" (John 18:11). Now, at long last, the ordeal of suffering had been endured, and that cup had been drained. The will of God had been fulfilled. What Jesus now longed for was to return to God. Thirsty? Yes, the physical suffering was certainly real. But there was another thirst, a thirst of a different kind, and on a different plane: a thirst for God (*Friday Afternoon*, London: Epworth Press, 1976, pp. 88f.).

Here, as at every level of his suffering on the cross, Jesus is representative of all humankind. There are moments, fleeting perhaps, when we find ourselves longing for God. Many of us have known times when the limitations of the body with its weakness, its sickness, even its willful passions, have come between us and God. Jesus expresses for us this inner sense of searching for the infinite. But he also fulfills it. Across the ages Christians have testified that he who promised "Blessed are those who hunger and thirst for righteousness, for they will be filled" (Matt. 5:6) has through his cross become the road to the loving heart of God where all such hungering and thirsting is fully satisfied.

I have a treasured bookmark in my Bible given to me by an elderly lady on which is an embroidered text. Looked at from one side it is an unsightly mixture of threads and colors with no apparent meaning or design. When it is turned over, however, there can be seen in beautiful characters the words "God is love."

Seen from Good Friday, the cross is a confusing mixture of crushed hopes, human cruelty, and the defeat of goodness. But when it is seen with Easter eyes, it tells a different story. It tells of love that would not stop loving; of God embracing the whole of human experience with all its ugliness, its pain, and its sin; of love refusing to give up but believing that even in the darkest hate some spark of love might respond to need; of a deep longing for God that even the most terrible spiritual darkness could not extinguish.

There is in Samoa a road with an interesting story and a special name, because of the distinguished author Robert Louis Stevenson. At one point in this island's history he intervened to effect the release of some imprisoned Samoan chiefs. Once out of prison, instead of hurrying home to their families, the released men, moved by deep regard and gratitude, made their way up the hill to the famous writer's house. Squatting in a circle on the dining-room floor, they announced that they intended to express their gratitude to the one whom they called "Tusitala" (writer of tales) by building a road from his house to the public highway. It was a large undertaking involving the felling of many trees and the removal of large boulders. When it was completed, the chiefs insisted that it be called *Alo Loto Alofa*, "The Road of the Loving Heart" (Joseph W. Ellison, *Tusitala of the South Seas*, Hastings House, 1953, pp. 264-65).

When seen with Easter eyes, the cruel cross of rejection and suffering is transformed into the road of the loving heart of God. In Jesus, God has entered fully into our humanity. In Jesus, God has shown that he never gives up on any of us. In Jesus, he has shown that those who truly thirst for him will find in the mystery of the cross the means whereby their deep longing, their thirst for God, may be quenched.

Study Questions

1. Read Lamentations 1:12. In an age when we know of terrible sufferings inflicted by one group of human beings upon another, is the suffering of Jesus different? If so, in what ways were his suffering and sorrow unique?

2. Read Isaiah 52:13–53:12. In what way do you understand Jesus to have been "wounded for our transgressions." What is your understanding of chapter 53, verse 10?

3. Do you find the thought of God sharing in our grief and pain to be helpful? If so, how does it help in coping with your own suffering or that of others you know? How can you use this part of the Christian revelation to help those who are going through hurtful experiences?

4. What has helped you most when you have experienced a time of bereavement or grief? What is your strategy for helping others in similar circumstances? How does the cross and the suffering of Christ influence what you have to say to a parent whose child is terminally ill or someone whose loved one has been the victim of wanton violence?

5. We believe Jesus never gives up on anyone. Have there been occasions when you or someone you know has been unable to find goodness in another person? Consider ways of coping with this challenge to faith and evangelism.

6. What practical steps are you taking in your devotional life to cultivate those moments when you truly hunger and thirst after God? What means have you found most helpful in satisfying that inner longing and need?

Focus for the Week: Sharing Christ's Suffering

Spend a short period each day this week meditating on the various accounts of the crucifixion in the Four Gospels. Also reflect on Hebrews 4:15 and Philippians 2:1-11. A Spiritual asks, "Were *you* there when they crucified my Lord?" Imagine that you actually were there and also bear in mind that the sins that took Jesus to the cross lurk too often in your heart. Each day this week, imagine yourself to be a different part of the scene: on one day, part of the crowd, on another, one of the soldiers, then one of the disciples, then one of the malefactors. Try to share in some small measure in the suffering of Jesus (see Phil. 3:10). Ask the question, "Lord is it I? Am I the one who betrayed you?" and allow your heart and conscience to give an honest reply.

The Seventh Week in Lent
Fear and Joy (Easter People)

"He is not here; for he has been raised, as he said. Come, see the place where he lay. Then go quickly and tell his disciples, 'He has been raised from the dead, and indeed he is going ahead of you to Galilee; there you will see him.' This is my message for you." So they left the tomb quickly with fear and great joy, and ran to tell his disciples. (Matt. 28:6-8)

It was at the beginning of Holy Week some years ago when I received a letter that I still treasure. The writer, Dr. W. E. Sangster, was a friend whom I had admired ever since I came to faith. For months the voice of this great preacher had been silent because of a progressive illness. In his encouraging letter he said, "It is a terrible thing to be *unable* to stand in a pulpit on Easter Sunday and say 'Christ is risen,' but I can think of something much worse. That is to stand in a pulpit on Easter Sunday and NOT to say Christ is risen."

Easter Sunday is the great day of the Christian year and the one toward which all our Lenten journey has been directed. On it we want to shout, "The Lord is risen indeed!" Without it everything we believe and celebrate would be meaningless. Because of it life and death have been completely transformed.

With two thousand years of Christian history behind us, it is almost impossible for us to realize that the first Easter began sad and hopeless for those dispirited disciples. Dawn was casting its eerie half-light on the rocks and trees as two sorrowing women emerged from their homes to carry out a labor of grief and love. Two days earlier, because of the approaching Sabbath, they had watched as the body of Jesus was hastily wrapped in a linen cloth and laid in a tomb hewn out of the rock (Matt. 27:59-61). Now they came in the gray twilight of the first day of the week to perform a last act of devotion. Their mission, to embalm the body.

Terrible things had happened in the past three days that had shaken the foundations of their lives. At the cross they had seen what had been done to the one they loved. They had witnessed the disgrace, the cruelty, and the insults. They had also seen the love that would not stop loving. Fear and grief must have filled their hearts as they made their way to that cold grave.

And then they had a strange, bewildering, inexpressible experience. They found the grave empty and were told that Jesus had been raised from the dead. They ran to tell the disciples the news, and Matthew adds, "They left the tomb quickly with fear and great joy."

We can understand the joy, but what seems strange, at first, is to read that they also experienced fear. But on reflection, was it so remarkable? This was not the kind of fear we associate with terror or ignorance but rather a fear that is better understood as awe. It was the handmaid of worship. They had been confronted with something entirely new that challenged all their understanding and belief, and they were awestruck. And in the midst of our Easter celebration, amid all our gladness and rejoicing, we may miss the true glory and full wonder of the festival if we do not pause to share their awe. Consider the implications of this momentous event, the like of which earth had not witnessed before and after which nothing could be the same again.

Our understanding of Jesus has been changed by the Resurrection.

F. Warburton Lewis in *Jesus, Savior of Men* (London: Epworth Press, 1949, pp. 203f.) offers an illuminating insight. He reminds us that when John wrote his Gospel, it was his original intention to conclude with the Resurrection story in chapter 20 and that his material had been carefully selected with a particular climax in mind (John 20:30-31). Within this chapter there is a carefully orchestrated spirit of expectancy. First, Mary discovers that the stone has been rolled from the tomb. She dashes to tell Peter and John. Immediately these two disciples run to the tomb and discover that the body of Jesus has disappeared. Next Jesus appears to Mary in the garden. She immediately tells the disciples she has seen the Lord. Then in the evening Jesus comes to the assembled disciples, blesses them with his peace, and reveals his scars.

Now the scene is set. John has completed his preparations and is ready to raise the curtain on the glorious climax of the drama. And then we have a surprise. The final piece in John's unfolding of the Resurrection story, the great finale to this most carefully composed Gospel, is the revelation to Thomas!

It seems incongruous. Thomas is the epitome of doubt. How can this be a fitting end to the greatest story ever told? Is it possible that this only seems strange to us because we have misunderstood the significance of his story and the nature of his doubt? Warburton Lewis thinks so.

Could it be that Thomas, having loved the Master with a rare and desperate devotion, had not only been torn apart by the agony of Christ's suffering at Calvary but had also, in a strange, painful, yet wonderful way been uplifted by what to him had been an incredible demonstration of his Master's love? Had he been overwhelmed by the loving, suffering, dying Christ of the cross? Were this so, the excited disciples with their story that Jesus was alive would have been bewildering and even disturbing. His mind would have been in turmoil. If Jesus were alive, did this mean that Calvary and all the suffering love that had entranced him there was not real but was just a phantom experience? Thomas was familiar with the many legends that abounded in the world of his day of gods who were alleged to have lived on earth, who had seemed to die, and who then had miraculously returned to life. All these legends had happy endings. Were his friends fantasizing about Jesus with such a story?

The violence of his language, which jars us at first, indicates the terrible agony of his mind. The suffering he saw at Calvary was real. The nails were real. The spear was real. The blood and the pain were real. And nothing, absolutely nothing, was going to turn that dreadful yet exalting experience into a fantasy. His words at first appear ugly. They are certainly not the kind that people use unless there are powerful emotions at work within: "Unless I see the mark of the nails in his hands, *and put my finger in the mark of the nails and my hand in his side,* I will not believe" (John 20:25, emphasis mine).

The very things we would expect the Resurrection to have erased, the marks of shame and humiliation, are precisely what Thomas wanted to see. And Jesus responded to this need of Thomas by showing his wounds. The sight of them silenced the apostle's doubts. The scars overwhelmed him. Here was no legend, no fantasy. This was glorious, incredible, terrifying truth. Thomas, overcome with awe, with Easter fear, becomes the very first person in history to make the great confession: "My Lord and my God!" (John 20:28). Here in the words of Thomas is the climax of the Gospel. Now John's task is done, and he can lay down his pen. The story has been fully told. Through the eyes and lips of Thomas we reach the heart of Easter: *God was himself on the cross.*

Millions who have not had the advantage of seeing Jesus as Thomas saw him, have nevertheless followed that disciple and have become Easter people by joining him in hailing Jesus as God incarnate. Here is good reason for awe. The Resurrection affirms that the Jesus of the Galilean road is God in human form. "For in him all the fullness of God was pleased to dwell" (Col. 1:19). Easter changes our understanding of Jesus. No longer can he be confined to human categories. Titles such as teacher, healer, and prophet only express a small part of the mystery of Christ's person; they all fall short. Only the confession of Thomas is adequate: "My Lord and my God."

The disciples were changed by the Resurrection.

The most telling evidence of the Resurrection is not the discovery of the empty tomb, nor the powerful testimony of the New Testament writers, but the transformation of the disciples. They were awed by the realization that because Jesus had conquered death and was living and present with them, they now in some terrifying yet exhilarating way could be the channels of God's love and power. This was enough to fill them with fear and great joy!

They assumed a new daring audacity. Instead of cringing indoors in secret, they were on the streets glorying in their allegiance to the one whom the authorities had crucified. Danger no longer daunted them. It was as though they had suddenly entered a completely new world filled with the presence of Christ. They would understand the testimony of Saul Kane, the converted prizefighter whom the poet John Masefield describes on the morning after his spiritual awakening:

> O glory of the lighted mind.
> How dead I'd been, how dumb, how blind.
> The station brook, to my new eyes,
> Was babbling out of Paradise,
> The waters rushing from the rain
> Were singing Christ has risen again.
> I thought all earthly creatures knelt
> From rapture of the joy I felt.
> (*Poems*, New York: Macmillan, 1929, p. 88)

Death has been changed by the Resurrection.

Death was the ultimate conqueror. The end of all human endeavor. All dreams, hopes, and fears ended with the grave.

But the first Easter changed it all. The Salvation Army has a lovely phrase that they use when one of their members dies. That person, they say, has been "promoted to glory." It has a triumphant and a scriptural ring about it that Easter people echo in their hearts. Consider again those two women coming early to the tomb. They brought with them an understanding of God that, although enlarged by Jesus, was still the product of their tradition and upbringing. Their devotion was beyond question. But until that moment they had not realized the immensity, the incomprehensibility of God's greatness. Then, at the open grave there dawns upon them the realization that even the most fearful of all the enemies, death, was no match for God. "And they left the tomb quickly with fear and great joy."

The resurrection of Jesus changes our whole concept of death. It affirms that the deep, instinctive conviction that death is not the end of the story but only the end of the first chapter is not wishful thinking; it is rooted in the heart of God. The Resurrection affirms that our sense of beauty and morality, our quest for truth, and our love of others does not end when our hearts stop beating. These qualities have eternal value. The victory of Christ over death brings with it the blessed hope that we will see our loved ones again. It affirms that because Jesus is alive, eternal life is an experience into which we can enter now (John 17:3) and that this Easter experience is beyond the reach of the cold hand of death.

Henry Scott Holland, former Canon of St. Paul's and Regius Professor of Divinity at Oxford University, in a sermon entitled "The King of Terrors" in *Facts of the Faith* (Longmans, Green and Co., 1919, p. 126), speaks of this new attitude toward death that Easter people possess as they gaze at a loved one who has passed into the more immediate presence of God:

> And what the face says in its sweet silence to us as a last message from the one whom we loved is: "Death is nothing at all. It does not count. I have only slipped away into the next room. Nothing has happened. Everything remains exactly as it was. I am I, and you are you, and the old life that we lived so fondly together is untouched, unchanged. Whatever we were to each other, that we still are. Call me by the old familiar name. Speak to me in the easy way which you always used. Put no difference into your tone. Wear no forced air of solemnity or sorrow. Laugh as we always laughed at the little jokes that we enjoyed together. Play, smile, think of me, pray for me. Let my name be the household word that it always was. Let it be spoken without an effort, without the ghost of a shadow upon it. Life means all that it ever meant. It is the same as it ever was. There is absolute and unbroken continuity. What is this death but a negligible accident? Why should I be out of mind because I am out of sight? I am but waiting for you, for an interval, somewhere very near, just around the corner. All is well. Nothing is hurt; nothing is lost. One brief moment and all will be as it was before. How we shall laugh at the trouble of parting when we meet again!"

Here is the triumphant joy and awe that characterizes the faith of Easter people. It is both glorious and awesome to know that death, the final enemy, has been conquered. The Resurrection becomes the foundation stone of our faith. Luke tells us that "with great power the apostles gave their testimony to the resurrection of the Lord Jesus, and great grace was upon them all" (Acts 4:33). This must ever be the task of Easter people. The joy and gladness of Easter is blended with a holy awe. Awe because we now see Jesus as God incarnate. Awe because we now know that timid, frightened men and women such as we can, through the living presence of Christ, be transformed into powerful agents for God's kingdom in a hostile world. Awe because death has been swallowed up in victory.

Are we Easter people?

Study Questions

1. Read John 11:17-44. What was so different about the resurrection of Jesus that transformed his disciples, whereas the resurrection of Lazarus did not?

2. The risen Christ enters every situation with us. Are there areas in your life where he would not be welcome or where his presence would embarrass you? What do you plan to do about them?

3. Jesus was very selective in his resurrection appearances. He did not appear to his enemies. Wouldn't such an appearance have been a means of convincing them of the truth of his teaching? Why do you think he withheld his risen presence from them?

4. Read Luke 24:13-32. (a) Note verses 25-27. What do you think would have been some of the things to which Jesus would have drawn attention as he expounded the scriptures? (b) Note verses 30-31. What do you think made the two disciples aware that their guest was Jesus? Why do you think they did not recognize him immediately?

5. Read 1 Corinthians 15:3-8, 20-22. Do we concentrate so much on physical life that we neglect the eternal dimension? What evidence of this can you cite? Can you say that "death is nothing at all" or honestly ask the question, "Where, O death, is your victory?" (1 Cor. 15:55). What steps can we take so that we make the risen Christ the center of our lives and become Easter people? What specific things will you do?

Focus for the Week: Sharing the Joy of Easter

This is a time of celebration. Consider all the good things in your life, your home, your church, and your community that are due to the presence of the risen Christ. Recall with thanksgiving that because of Easter, you are surrounded by a cloud of witnesses; dear ones bound to you by ties of kin, affection, or faith who are now with Christ in glory. Share in the Easter joy that "death has been swallowed up in victory" (1 Cor. 15:54).

May the radiance of our lives declare to all who meet us that we are Easter people!